MEETING JUDITH SHEINDLIN

AN ENTHRALLING BIOGRAPHY

LIZA MICHAEL

Copyright@2023

LIZA MICHAEL

ALL RIGHTS RESERVED

CONTENTS

1. **INTRODUCTION**

2. **THE FORMATIVE YEARS OF JUDITH SHEINDLIN'S**

   Childhood
   Education

3. **THE PROGRESSION OF SHEINDLIN'S PROFESSIONAL CAREER**

   At the Bar
   Joining the Bench
   Manhattan family court
   The TV Show
   Net Worth
   Recognitions and Awards
   Publications

4. **A BRIEF SYNOPSIS OF THE BOOKS WRITTEN BY THE INCREDIBLE JUDGE**

   Win or Lose by How You Choose
   Beauty Fades, Dumb Is Forever
   Don't pee on my leg and then try to convince me that it's raining
   You Can't Judge a Book by its Cover: Cool Rules for School
   Keep It Simple, Stupid

5. **INSIDE JUDITH SHEINDLIN'S PERSONAL LIFE**

   Ronald Levy
   Jerry Sheindlin
   The Hard Feelings of Lose
   Love Over Everything

Business Endeavors
Some Personal Positions

6. CONTROVERSIES STOKED BY JUDITH SHEINDLIN OVER THE COURSE OF HER CAREER

Behind the Gavel
Sheindlin Was Being Sued Over an Accused China Scheme
Adam Levy and the Legal Maze
The Feud with Sands

7. CONCLUSION

1. INTRODUCTION

Judith Sheindlin is a shining light in both the history of American law and the fascinating realm of reality television.

The television show called "Judge Judy" catapulted her to stardom. The program premiered in 1996 and quickly became a staple for legal fans around the country, forever cementing Judy's name in living rooms from coast to coast.

However, Judy's background dates back far before the lure of the little screen. She started her formal legal education at American University's Washington

College of Law. She was the only female candidate among a group of 126 men. She went on to New York Law School and added it to her list of accomplishments thereafter.

In 1982, the then-Mayor of New York City, Ed Koch, recognized her extraordinary skill and presented her with a gavel and bench. As the years progressed, her aggressive yet fair attitude in the courtroom was highlighted by the television program "60 Minutes" in 1993.

Judy's first experience in the judicial system was in a family court, when her candor, charm, and passionate nature made her the talk of the halls.

Outside of the court, her charisma and beauty made her a television star. The pen, too, jigged to her ideas, and soon she was surrounded by volumes on parenting, ethics, and the whole spectrum of human experience. Television icons from "Good Morning America" to "Jimmy Kimmel Live" praised her one-of-a-kind personality, while prestigious newspapers like USA Today, *The New York Times*, and *The Wall Street Journal* gushed over her.

However, success and recognition didn't always come easily. And in the intricate field of law, she had her fair share of difficult cases to contend with. In 2011, during a shooting, Judy had a fright when she fainted from a ministroke. Despite the challenges she faced, Judith Sheindlin's reputation remains unshaken; she is remembered as a pioneer in the fields of law and show business.

Today, Judge Judy Sheindlin is a symbol of steadfast authority and no-holds-barred honesty in the big world of courtroom TV. Her rapid rise to fame has made her a common name. Some people like her, others don't, but millions of people watch her anyway. She has been getting people's attention for decades with the way she does justice, which is different from many other judges. But beyond the studio's stage-like atmosphere and the prepared reality is a page full of stories that are more interesting, complicated, and often deeper than any episode of her show that we watch. This book invites readers to this page and gives them an honest look at the life of their TV's famous judge.

This story not only follows Sheindlin's career path but also goes deep into her personal path. As we learn more about the controversies surrounding Sheindlin's alleged wrongdoings at work, we also delve into her family ties that are complicated by the law and see her in situations where she is not behind the bench but in front of it, we get a clear picture of the contradictions of fame, the difficulties of public life, and the never-ending search for the truth.

This story takes us into the world of fame and raises important questions about the responsibilities of those who are always in the spotlight. It looks at the sacrifices that have to be made, the identities that are at risk, and the constant scrutiny that comes with being a public figure with a lot of power.

This book also gives us a front-row seat to a world where real life is often more interesting than fiction, where lines blur and the real and the fake are hard to tell apart.

Join us as we go beyond the courtroom and into a maze where every turn reveals a new facet, a new challenge, and a truth that never changes: Justice, in all its forms, is a pursuit that is full of both public and private trials, and even a judge, with all her knowledge, is not safe from them.

2. THE FORMATIVE YEARS OF JUDITH SHEINDLIN'S

Childhood

On October 21, 1942, a very special person named Judith Susan Blum came into the world on a crisp fall day. She came to the busy city of Brooklyn, which is right in the middle of New York City. The threads of Judith's German-Jewish and Russian-Jewish background were sewn together to make a patchwork of two cultures.

Murray Blum and Ethel Silverman, her parents, were brave people who left their home countries to find a better life in

America. Murray was born in Germany, but Ethel was born and raised in Russia. They brought with them the rich Jewish customs and beliefs, which they passed on to their children with love.

While growing up, Judith had the greatest respect for her parents and loved the things that made each of them special. In her eyes, her father was nothing short of amazing, and his appearance was like the creation of sliced bread. Judith's heart will always remember how wise, strong, and loving he was. Her mother, on the other hand, was a simple and sensible woman who was very down-to-earth. Judith liked to call her "a meat and potatoes kind of gal," which shows how grounded her mother was.

At the Blum house, Judith grew up with three brothers, all of whom she loved very much. As the only girl in her family, she learned to get along in the world by being strong and determined. She made her own way into a home full of loud laughs and fun banter.

Education

As the years went by, Judith went to James Madison High School, a well-known school in the streets of Brooklyn, to finish her secondary education. She did not stop wanting to learn, so she started a new part of her life at American University, which is in the city of Washington, District of Columbia. After working hard for years, she was happy to get a Bachelor of Arts degree in 1963. She studied the complexities of government. In a group of 126 students, Judith showed how determined and strong she was.

She later went to New York Law School, in the middle of New York City, to get a law degree because she wanted to learn more and help people. With determination, she engaged herself in the world of law. In 1965, she got her Juris Doctor, which shows how dedicated she was and how smart she was. She passed the difficult bar test and is now a qualified lawyer in the state of New York.

Going forward, she got honorary Doctor of Law degrees from prestigious schools like Elizabethtown College in Pennsylvania, University at Albany SUNY, and New York Law School. These degrees were given to her because of her many accomplishments and services to society. These honors were a sign of how hard she worked and how determined she was to do what she loved.

So, the amazing story of Judith Susan Blum, who was born into a world with many different cultures and endless possibilities, keeps getting better and better, leaving a lasting mark. Her journey gives us hope and reminds us that if we work hard and stay strong, we can solve any problem and make a difference in the world that will last.

3. THE PROGRESSION OF SHEINDLIN'S PROFESSIONAL CAREER

At the Bar

In 1965, Judith Sheindlin started her legal job as a business lawyer at a cosmetics company. However she did not like this job, so she decided to focus on raising her two kids. Within two years, she quit her job so she could spend more time with her family.

Joining the Bench

In 1972, Sheindlin joined a family court and began a new part of her law work. After a while, New York City Mayor Edward Koch took notice of her. In 1982, he made her a judge in the criminal court at the Bronx branch of the family court.

Manhattan family court

Four years later, in 1986, Sheindlin was given the job of Supervising Judge in the part of the Manhattan family court that dealt with children. Many people liked and respected her direct personality and no-nonsense way of doing things, which gave her power in the courts.

In February 1993, the Los Angeles Times wrote a story about Sheindlin that called her a "legal superheroine." Because of this, she was on an episode of 60

Minutes, which is a well-known news show on TV. This brought Sheindlin to the forefront of the law field.

The TV Show

After Judith Sheindlin retired from being a judge in 1996, she was asked to be the star of a new courtroom TV show that would show real cases and decisions. She said yes, and on September 16, 1996, the first episode of "Judge Judy" aired on TV stations across the country. Sheindlin quickly became a star because of how popular the show was.

Sheindlin became well-known for her part as Judge Judy, in which she was known for her quick wit and no-nonsense attitude. The show was always the most popular court show on TV, and its numbers kept going up from year to year, which was a big deal in the history of television. It was watched by an average of 10 million people every day, most of whom were women aged 25 to 54.

Sheindlin's deal was extended more than once because the show kept doing well and people kept watching. She was still committed to the show as of the 17th season, which started in 2012-2013. Sheindlin said that it was hard for her to leave the show because she still liked what she was doing and had a loyal audience.

Net Worth

Because of how well Sheindlin did on TV, he made a lot of money. In 2005, she made $25 million a year in the U.S., and in 2007, her net worth was reported to be $95 million. Forbes' list of the top 20 richest women in the entertainment business put her at number 13. Her wages went up even more when her deal was extended in 2010. The show's production is said to cost $45 million per year.

Recognitions and Awards

Sheindlin's role as Judge Judy has been referenced in various television programs, including Will & Grace, NBC's The Weakest Link, and The Academy Awards. Her influence extended to literature as well, with Jon Stewart mentioning her in his book America: A Citizen's Guide to Democracy Inaction. Sheindlin has also participated in numerous cable news interviews.

In 2015, she received the Woman of the 21st Century Award from the Women's Guild and was recognized by the Guinness World Records for having the longest career as a Television Judge.

In 2014, Sheindlin was the recipient of The Mary Pickford Award.

In 2013, she was appointed as the vice president of the law society at University College Dublin, recognizing her significant contributions to family law.

In 2012, she received the VP/LAW Society prize from University College Dublin.

In 2010, Sheindlin was presented with the prestigious Brandon Tartikoff Legacy Award.

In 2006, she was honored with a Star on the Hollywood Walk of Fame and received the Gracie Allen Tribute Award from the American Women in Radio and Television.

Her television program, "Judge Judy," was honored with a Daytime Emmy Award in June 2013.

Her contributions to the field of law were recognized when she received the

Distinguished Alumni Award from New York Law School in 2000.

Due to her rising fame, Sheindlin was invited to serve as a judge for the Miss America Pageant in 1999.

Publications

Sheindlin has written several books in addition to her work on TV. "Do not Pee on My Leg and Tell Me It is Raining," Sheindlin's first book, came out in 1996. During her 25-year run as a judge in family court, she oversaw more than 20,000 cases. But it was in the same year that her book came out, that Sheindlin chose to give up being a judge.

After her third book came out, Sheindlin kept putting out more work. At the beginning of the 2000s, she put out a book called "Win or Lose by How You Choose." It was meant to teach kids how to make good choices. The next year, she wrote a book called "You Can not Judge a Book by Its Cover." It was about family and morals. In 2000, she wrote another book called "Keep It Simple, Stupid." It was called "You Are Smarter Than You Look," and it gave tips on how to solve common family fights. "Keep It Simple, Stupid" became a best-seller on the New York Times list.

In 2010, Sheindlin published two more books: "What Would Judy Say" and "What Would Judy SayIn these books, she kept sharing her ideas and tips.

Sheindlin's fame also led to her being on Saturday Night Live, Celebrity Profile, Headliners & Legends on MSNBC, Biography on A&E, and Intimate Portrait on Lifetime Television, among others.

In 2011, Sheindlin passed out while shooting her show and was taken to the hospital for a short time. No one knows what caused her to pass out, but she was sent home the next day after being held overnight.

So, Judith Sheindlin's legal career took her from business law to family court, where she made a big difference and became known for her no-nonsense approach to the law.

4. A BRIEF SYNOPSIS OF THE BOOKS WRITTEN BY THE INCREDIBLE JUDGE

Win or Lose by How You Choose

In her first book written just for young readers, Sheindlin offers a unique way for parents and children to talk about making decisions and moral judgments. The book has 36 multiple-choice questions with no answers and comments from the author for both adults and children.

In each question, the main character faces a problem, and then there are four different ways to solve it. The choices were made to be unclear on purpose so that in some cases, there could be more than one right answer. The parent's job is to talk to their child and help them choose the best way based on their own values and advice.

One possible situation is when someone knocks on the door and you can either ignore them or ask who they are before letting them in. The right answer rests on what the child's parent tells him or her to do. In this case, it is interesting that Sheindlin does not force her own choice on anyone or explain how she made her decision.

The book is written so that an adult and a child can read it together and talk about it and think about it. Tore's cartoon line drawings are fun and add a lighthearted touch to the book, making it more interesting for kids.

Sheindlin wrote this book for kids ages 7 to 12 because she wants to help them deal with the problems they face and give them a place to learn and grow in a healthy way.

Beauty Fades, Dumb Is Forever

Sheindlin's no-nonsense manner and straightforward approach to life come through in her work, just as they do on her TV show.

Sheindlin tells personal stories and talks about events from her work all through the book. These stories give the reader useful insights and tips. She talks about the problems she faced as a woman in fields controlled by men and gives advice on how to deal with them. She also talks about her own marriages and divorces and gives honest thoughts about her own life.

Sheindlin talks about her "Hoover File," which is a list of compliments and things she did well that helped her get reappointed to the bench. Sheindlin's honesty and lack of self-consciousness when sharing such details make her story seem more real.

If you have seen Sheindlin's TV show, you will notice that her unique style and attitude come through in her work. Fans of her show will enjoy reading the book more because they can hear her voice as she says the words.

Overall, Sheindlin's book is a mix of history and useful advice. It gives readers a look at her life and work and tells them how to do well in tough situations.

Don't pee on my leg and then try to convince me that it's raining

Sheindlin has been in charge of the Manhattan Family Court as the chief judge for ten years. In that time, she has built a reputation for being able to cut through the fog of legal and government words with sharp clarity. This fierce honesty comes through in her powerful book, whose title seems to have been chosen with a sharp, purposeful edge.

Getlin, who works for the Los Angeles Times and is a reporter, helps her with this plan. Sheindlin paints a picture of a society on the verge of collapse. This is mostly because of a subtle shift: people are putting less emphasis on personal duty and more on government roles. She paints a picture of a society where people's responsibilities are moving away from them and onto larger systems.

She lays out the problems with the current system and then goes into detail about how it affects the average taxpayer's finances. Sheindlin gets to the bottom of why people in modern America are losing their sense of duty and honesty.

Even though she has good ideas, she doesn't give advice with a full action plan. Her call to action is clear: people need to have self-discipline, take care of their duties, and act with honesty. In effect, Sheindlin's message is a call for people to get back to basic principles like honesty and personal responsibility.

You Can't Judge a Book by its Cover: Cool Rules for School

It is more than just a book. It's a guide, a way to start a conversation, and a way for young people to learn more about the world around them. It's Judge Judy's way of reaching out to younger people and teaching them the morals and principles she's been fighting for all her life.

The main goal of the book is to help kids build a strong sense of right and wrong. By putting real-world events in a school setting, it tries to give kids the tools they need to make good choices and deal with the many challenges of school life.

Like in her other children's books, Judge Judy sets up problems and gives readers several options for how to handle them. This structure is fun for kids because it makes them think and think about the choices they make. But in "You Can't Judge a Book by Its Cover: Cool Rules for School," Judge Judy doesn't give a clear "right" answer for each situation. Instead, she supports talks, preferably with adults like parents or teachers, to help the child come to a moral and ethical decision.

Judith Sheindlin, beyond what she does on TV, she has shown a strong desire to teach moral lessons and give ethical advice, especially to kids. The book is meant to give kids advice on how to deal with different events they might face at school. Through a number of events, it helps people think about what they should do in different conditions. For example, it might talk about how to deal with bullies, how to share with peers, and how to tell the truth. The book's illustrations were done by Bob Tore. They give the book a visual draw and help break down and picture the lessons and stories that Judge Judy tells.

Keep It Simple, Stupid

In this book, Sheindlin is back on the literary stage, bringing with her the same mix of wit and knowledge that made her famous thanks to her hit TV show. She tells the story of age-old family fights she has seen in her long and successful work through vivid stories. No subject is off-limits, from the breakup of couples who lived together to the details of planning a funeral.

In "Keep It Simple, Stupid," Sheindlin tells people how to deal with some of life's most usual problems and pitfalls. She tells stories from her own life and from her work as a lawyer to show how to handle difficult situations by keeping things simple and straightforward.

The book talks about a lot of different things, from personal relationships and family interactions to law issues and problems in society. It's written in the normal way of Judge Judy, which means it's direct, sharp, and often funny.

Sheindlin also tells stories about how people can make things worse when they overcomplicate things or don't take responsibility for what they do. These stories not only show what goes on behind the scenes of her TV show, but they also show what can happen when you don't keep things simple.

The book is not just a book about the law or about how to get along with other people. It's a call to action for readers to believe in their own intelligence, use common sense, and face the difficulties of life with a clear and simple mind. For people who like Judge Judy's TV show, the book has more of the honest advice and sharp wit that they have come to enjoy. For some, it's a good lesson that sometimes the easiest answers are the best ones.

Every story has the same rhythm as her courtroom: everyone gets a chance to be in the spotlight and say what they want.

But, in true Judge Judy style, once they've made their cases, she walks firmly into the fight and gives out her own brand of justice. Those who are stubborn enough to make family fights, she calls "inconsiderate" or "downright shallow." Her vocal scoldings are famous, but they're just one way she gets back at people. She also uses actions like wrist slaps and sharp, tongue-in-cheek comments.

Still, the book has its way of looking at things that are exciting. In the case of a nasty split, she might agree to formal parenting rights. Still, Sheindlin never hesitates to question the letter of the law when it goes against a child's real well-being, asking for kinder, more sympathetic answers.

With the book, her fans, who are many and very faithful, know and respect her lasting support for honesty. They also know how much she hates lying and betrayal, and they know that bad people shouldn't expect her to forgive them.

Judge Judy doesn't just point out the problems that get people stuck in money, love, breaking up, and getting back together. Instead, she holds her readers to a higher standard, telling them to let go of childish things, grow up, and always choose the right thing to do.

5. INSIDE JUDITH SHEINDLIN'S PERSONAL LIFE

Ronald Levy

Judy Sheindlin married Ronald Levy in the spring of 1964 when everything was blooming. Jamie Hartwright and Adam Levy, their two children, came into their lives at the same time. Judy's job was just getting off the ground when things changed. She was at an intersection, like many women of her age, so she decided to be a mother and put her dreams of becoming a lawyer on hold for a while.

Judy was an unbending force in court, a storm that didn't take any nonsense. But under that tough exterior was a heart that longed for the love of family and the success of a career. She was sure that if she worked hard and stayed committed, she could be in both worlds because they were the two bases of her universe

During an honest interview with Fox News, Judy talked about how the waves kept pulling her and Ronald apart. It hurt that Ronald didn't understand her desire to get back into her career and would often brush it off as a hobby. Over time, Judy came to realize that Ronald, like many men of his time, might not have been ready for his life to change. The waves of time kept moving, and in 1976, after 12 happy years together, the pair chose to split up.

Jerry Sheindlin

In 1978, Judy met Jerry Sheindlin because of the strange ways that life works.

Fate often has funny ideas, and it had a cool plan for how Judy and Jerry would meet for the first time. In a busy bar for lawyers, they ran into each other. At that time, Jerry, the tough lawyer for the defense, and Judy, the tough lawyer for the prosecution, were on different sides of the court. Jerry was having a lively conversation with a writer from the New York Post when Judy, who was never one to be shy, walked up to him, playfully touched his face, and asked who he was. Jerry was surprised by her boldness, so he told her in a firm voice to step back, calling her "Lady." Still, there was an unsaid spark beneath this abrupt meeting.

In the aftermath, Judy told Katie Couric a story about how Jerry's charm and those shiny shoes made her fall in love with him. On the other hand, Jerry couldn't stay away from Judy because of how brave she was, which could have been a turnoff.

Even though the beginning was rough, their hearts found a beat. As they built a life together, the happiness of their five children was always the most important thing.

The Hard Feelings of Lose

Judy Sheindlin and her father, Dr. Murray Blum, had a deep and caring relationship in the middle of a lively community where stories and lives were linked. Dr. Blum, a well-known dentist, had been in love with

Judy's mother for 48 wonderful years. Judy got a deep-seated desire to be more and work harder from him. When she thought about the times they had spent together, she couldn't help but smile with a touch of longing, feeling the pull of hope her father might have helped her to grow. This link was so strong that when she first started being a judge, she wore his glasses so that he could be with her as she did her job.

But the year 1990 brought a storm that Judy hadn't seen coming, her father left the world. And as she tried to feel better, she could feel a rift between her and Jerry. She wanted Jerry to understand her and give her the comfort she needed in that rough sea of sadness. With her feelings running high, she thought about the lessons in the book "What Makes a Marriage Last" by Phil Donahue and Marlo Thomas. She then gave Jerry a choice, which he made clear in rushed divorce papers.

Love Over Everything

But the strength of love often surprises people. As the year 1991 began, the wind told stories of hope and second chances. While their time apart was a short break in the song of their lives, they were soon back together again. The old sayings were wise, you shouldn't teach a pig to sing, not because it would be pointless, but because it would make the pig mad. And she realized that sometimes it's best to just let love happen as it will. Jerry had to be Jerry, and not someone else.

In the big family of the Sheindlins, Judy took on the part of stepmother to Jerry's three children from a previous marriage with grace and love. Gregory, Jonathan, and Nicole were names that fit with the Sheindlin name. As the branches of their family tree grew, thirteen adorable grandkids came along and made their lives full of joy and laughter.

Business Endeavors

Not only is Sheindlin a family name, but it was also a business name. Adam Levy, Gregory, and Nicole all chose to wear the robes of the legal world, so they could be seen and heard in the halls of justice. Even though Jamie Hartwright and Jonathan Sheindlin chose to go into medicine to help people get better, the family was full of people who had done great things. The Her Honour Mentoring program, which Nicole and Judy came up with, was a big part of their success as a group. It showed how much they cared about helping the next generation.

Judy Sheindlin had a great job, but she also had the keys to many beautiful real estate properties. Her homes were all over the United States, from the wild plains of Wyoming to the sun-kissed beaches of Florida. Every two weeks, her job took her to Los Angeles, which was full of glitz and glitter. Here, among the dream-filled streets, she would tape scenes of her famous show, Judge Judy. She added a touch of luxury to her collection in 2013 when she bought a beautiful $10.7 million home in the heart of Beverly Hills. After a few years, in 2018, she and Jerry bought the beautiful Bird House in Newport, Rhode Island. This spacious 9,700-square-foot house was once owned by the famous Dorrance Hill Hamilton. It was nestled in a green 3.67 acres.

Some Personal Positions

Judy Sheindlin was happy to stitch her own unique design into political beliefs, not to be limited by any political party. Her voice was clear and easy to understand, just like the things she believed in.

Judy fought for love and equality, and she thought that two hearts could join together no matter what gender they were. She thought that the issue of same-sex marriage was too big for each state to handle on its own. Instead, she thought it needed a national answer.

Her view on government was different: she didn't like the idea of an all-powerful "big government," but she was sure that gun purchases should be more closely regulated.

Judy's journey through politics was marked by her ability to see things clearly. She didn't swear allegiance to party symbols. Instead, she swore loyalty to her views and ideals. Even though she had backed big names like Barack Obama in 2008 and giants like Ronald Reagan and Bill Clinton in their times, no one knew who she voted for in the 2012 presidential election.

In October 2019, Judy's political story took a turn she didn't expect. Before the world knew for sure that Michael Bloomberg wanted to run for president,

Judy's pen danced across the paper to write a letter of support for him. Her belief was strengthened when she went on to appear in an ad praising Bloomberg's character and accomplishments and painting him as a great leader.

6. CONTROVERSIES STOKED BY JUDITH SHEINDLIN OVER THE COURSE OF HER CAREER

Behind the Gavel

Judge Judy's sharp eyes have held people's attention for nearly thirty years. But with her show's huge success came rumors, theories, and later loud claims of scandals that seemed to cloud its memory.

More and more people were talking about whether or not "Judge Judy" was full of bad people. There were rumors that the set was a place where racism, lying, and a general bad vibe could be found. But how much of what is said in whispers and written down is true?

As 'Judge Judy' ended and rumors spread about Sheindlin's next project, many people couldn't help but wonder if it would carry on the bad reputation of its predecessor. Some people who used to be friends turned out to be haters and said that working on the set was like being in a pressure cooker. They pointed fingers and said that, even though Sheindlin didn't do it herself, she let a culture of discrimination and fear grow while she was in charge.

This wasn't a new accusation, which was scary. Since almost 20 years ago, both the news and court papers have expressed the same worries. Even though Judy wasn't the one who started it, these stories made it sound like she was a supporter who was completely unaware.

Then there's the powerful executive director Randy Douthit. There were rumors that he had done bad things, like make inappropriate comments or put Black defendants in the background. But Randy wasn't the only one in the spotlight. Other well-known people, like

Victoria Jenest and Amy Freisleben, were also mentioned in the rumors. Both were said to cause strife, use bullying, and maybe even do some inappropriate things on set.

But despite the storm of accusations, this trio didn't seem to be fazed as they moved from "Judge Judy" to the much-anticipated Amazon show. As the stories progress, one question remains: Where is the line between truth and fiction?

In the middle of the situation, her voice, which is usually a sign of power, seemed softer and more inward. She answered some of the complaints head-on, admitting that she might not have been as careful as she could have been as a leader. But it was surprising that she didn't get caught up in the charges that Randy, Victoria, and Amy were facing.

On the other hand, a representative for the famous TV judge took a different method and tried to highlight the loyalty and consistency in Sheindlin's working life. They brought up a shocking fact: three-quarters of the people who supported her on "Judge Judy" stayed with her on "Judy Justice." Many of these workers have been working with her for more than a decade or even a quarter of a century. They said that this kind of life was rare in the fast-paced world of television, which suggested that maybe things weren't as bad as they were made out to be.

But while Sheindlin's side tried to show that everyone was on the same side, Randy's legal team went on the attack. They asked Douthit for clarity and a strong rejection about the charges that were weighing him down. They claimed strongly that Randy was more than just his supposed mistakes and that, during his time on the show, he created a supportive, open, and productive workplace.

Sheindlin Was Being Sued Over an Accused China Scheme

Sheindlin was used to handing out punishments, but in March of 2013, the TV judge was facing some possible punishment of her own. As per reports, she was being sued for allegedly being sold fine china at a reduced price deal by her producer, when in reality, the fine china was worth significantly more than the value she got it for. It would appear that Sheindlin was being requested to return the china that she reportedly bought, with the suit alleging that the Christofle Mary Bone China was communal property, but that her producer, Randall Douthit, sold it to Judy for $50,000 when it true retail value is $514,421.14. The individual who made the claim was Douthit's ex-spouse, Patric Jones, who claimed that it was part of a plot Sheindlin and Douthit hatched in order to exclude her from the sale of what was she and her ex's common property. For her side, Sheindlin stated that she had not come across any complaint made by the previous Mrs. Douthit; yet, she did not owe this woman a single penny. According to Sheindlin, everyone would be in a significantly better position if this woman, who was 50 years old, would spend her time in a more productive manner by trying to obtain a job rather than abusing the judicial system with frivolous litigation.

Adam Levy and the Legal Maze

In the spring of 2013, people were talking and pointing fingers all over town. Adam Levy, not only was he facing legal charges, but he was also the son of the famous Judge Judy, Sheindlin.

The cases were as serious as they could get. Alexandru Hossu, a 35-year-old personal trainer who was known to the Levy family, was accused of a horrible crime: he raped a 12-year-old girl twice. As the story spread through the town, another fact came to light: Hossu was thought to have lived at Levy's house for a while.

Levy stepped away from the case because he knew how serious the charges were and how close he was to the person being charged. But Sheriff Donald Smith had a different point of view. He said that Levy was still trying to control what was going on, even though he said he was far away. From the sheriff's point of view, Levy's actions could be seen as not only unethical but also as an intentional attempt to get in the way of justice.

Well, instead of giving up, Levy fought back. He supported what his office did and said that it was right to do it at every step of the probe. In his mind, Sheriff Smith was just making fake charges and making things harder to figure out. This wasn't the first time they had a fight over something. In an earlier scene, they got into a fight over something as simple as traffic tickets.

As the dust settled, Hossu was locked up and waited for his day in court. Levy said that he had known Hossu for a long time, but he stressed that he was staying out of the case to avoid any appearance of bias.

But Sheindlin, an experienced judge and Levy's mother noticed that the town was losing sight of the real question: Was Hossu guilty of the crimes he was accused of? She thought that should have been the only thing that mattered, not the farce that had taken the spotlight.

The Feud with Sands

June 2004 wasn't just another month in the quiet town of Greenwich, Connecticut. A storm was coming, but it wasn't one of rain. Instead, it was one of disagreements and different ideas. At the center of it all was the star of "Judge Judy," who found herself on the other side of the courtroom bench, not as a judge but as an accuser.

The point of disagreement? A public playground is a symbol of fun, play, and maybe even innocence. But this field became a sign of problem and neglect for the Sheindlin family. They said that their neighbour Martin Sands broke the rules on purpose by building the sports field without the right permits. What went wrong? Erosion caused a river of muck to flow right into their clean swimming pool. It costs a crazy amount of money to clean: between $9,444 and $17,000.

When the local officials heard how worried the Sheindlin were, they stepped in. Martin Sands was told to stop everything from happening on the pitch until the right clearances were given. On the other hand, the girls' lacrosse team in their town was full of energy and excitement when their practice pitch was taken away from them. Their dreams were put on hold for a short time, which made their parents angry, but not at Sands but at the TV star and her family.

Yet, for the Sheindlins, who have ten sports-loving grandkids, the fight was about more than just a pitch or a pool. It was about a message or a way of life. They thought Sands was telling the young people a dangerous message: that rules could be broken if you had enough money. From the Sheindlin family's point of view, this wasn't just carelessness but a bad moral.

The town of Greenwich saw this fight, which was a scene of community ideals, individual rights, and the never-ending search for what's right.

7. CONCLUSION

Judy Sheindlin has proved her resiliency, drive, and devotion to making a difference both in her personal life and in her professional life through her various undertakings.

From the first pages, we start a deep look into the life of Judy Sheindlin, a figure who is just as mysterious as she is well-known. We've been through the ups and downs, the wins and losses, that come with a life in the spotlight. Now that the end is almost here, it's time to make sense of all the stories, arguments, and information that we have read.

Judy Sheindlin's life, both on and off camera, shows how fame can be both good and bad. Her solid presence on "Judge Judy" gave the show a unique style of justice that mixed human emotions with law decisions. But as we learned more, the complicated parts of her life and the lives of her closest relatives started to come out. From the fights in Greenwich to the rumored chaos behind the scenes of her show, we've seen that Sheindlin's life is just as detailed as the cases she was in charge of.

Also, the scandals that surrounded her, like the claims about the work environment on her show or the property battles, have shown how hard it can be to be famous. And because of what happened with her son Adam Levy in court, we've seen how family members of famous people are often under a lot more scrutiny, which blurs the line between the personal and the public.

In all these, Sheindlin's strength of character isn't just shown by how she deals with these problems. It shows how strong she is, how she can stand tall in times, and how strongly she sticks to her own version of the truth. Through decades in the public eye, her voice—firm and assertive—has rung with confidence, even when faced with hardship.

This book has not just been a study of one woman's life, but a deep look into the effects of fame, the ethical challenges of show business, and the relationships of family within the world of celebrity. As this story comes to an end, we know more about how the scales of justice work and how much weight they have. We've seen how these scales, which are important in a trial, are also a sign of the bigger sums we all try to find in life: between public image and personal truth.

We're not just ending Judy Sheindlin's story by putting this book down. Instead, we are left to think about our own ideas, judgments, and the many levels of truth that appear in the world around us. Through Sheindlin's story, challenges, and wins, we are reminded of the strength of the human spirit and the never-ending search for authenticity in a world full of fakes.

Made in United States
Orlando, FL
03 December 2023

40023832R00049